# RUNAWAYS

# RUNAWAYS
## DEAD END KIDS

WRITER: **JOSS WHEDON**

PENCILS: **MICHAEL RYAN**

INKS: **RICK KETCHAM** WITH **JAY LEISTEN** (#27), **ANDREW HENNESSY** (#29),
**VICTOR OLAZABA** (#30), **ROLAND PARIS** (#30) & **CRAIG YEUNG** (#30)

COLORS: **CHRISTINA STRAIN**

LETTERS: **VC's RANDY GENTILE** (#25), **JOE CARAMAGNA** (#26-27, #29-30)
& **CORY PETIT** (#28)

COVER ART: **JO CHEN**

ASSISTANT EDITOR: **DANIEL KETCHUM**

EDITOR: **NICK LOWE**

*RUNAWAYS* CREATED BY **BRIAN K. VAUGHAN** & **ADRIAN ALPHONA**

**RUNAWAYS VOL. 8: DEAD END KIDS.** Contains material originally published in magazine form as RUNAWAYS #25-30. Second edition. First printing 2017. ISBN# 978-1-302-90886-7. Published by MARVEL WORLDWIDE, INC., a subsidiary of MARVEL ENTERTAINMENT, LLC. OFFICE OF PUBLICATION: 135 West 50th Street, New York, NY 10020. Copyright © 2017 MARVEL No similarity between any of the names, characters, persons, and/or institutions in this magazine with those of any living or dead person or institution is intended, and any such similarity which may exist is purely coincidental. **Printed in the U.S.A.** DAN BUCKLEY, President, Marvel Entertainment; JOE QUESADA, Chief Creative Officer; TOM BREVOORT, SVP of Publishing; DAVID BOGART, SVP of Business Affairs & Operations, Publishing & Partnership; C.B. CEBULSKI, VP of Brand Management & Development, Asia; DAVID GABRIEL, SVP of Sales & Marketing, Publishing; JEFF YOUNGQUIST, VP of Production & Special Projects; DAN CARR, Executive Director of Publishing Technology; ALEX MORALES, Director of Publishing Operations; SUSAN CRESPI, Production Manager; STAN LEE, Chairman Emeritus. For information regarding advertising in Marvel Comics or on Marvel.com, please contact Vit DeBellis, Integrated Sales Manager, at vdebellis@marvel.com. For Marvel subscription inquiries, please call 888-511-5480. **Manufactured between 10/27/2017 and 11/27/2017 by QUAD/GRAPHICS WASECA, WASECA, MN, USA.**

10 9 8 7 6 5 4 3 2 1

COLLECTION EDITOR: JENNIFER GRÜNWALD
ASSISTANT EDITOR: CAITLIN O'CONNELL
ASSOCIATE MANAGING EDITOR: KATERI WOODY
EDITOR, SPECIAL PROJECTS: MARK D. BEAZLEY
VP PRODUCTION & SPECIAL PROJECTS: JEFF YOUNGQUIST
SVP PRINT, SALES & MARKETING: DAVID GABRIEL

EDITOR IN CHIEF: AXEL ALONSO
CHIEF CREATIVE OFFICER: JOE QUESADA
PRESIDENT: DAN BUCKLEY
EXECUTIVE PRODUCER: ALAN FINE

# DEAD-END KIDS

Tell me about the children.

Nico Minoru leads the, ah, "team". Child of the dark wizards, she now controls the Staff of One.

Adept at spells. Possibly not so much at leading.

Chase Stein, the oldest--all of eighteen. Despite his scientific pedigree, he's entirely dim.

His trump card is a mental bond with a... I don't want to say dinosaur...

Is it a dinosaur?

Most probably.

Then say it.

The animal belonged to the Yorkes' daughter, Gertrude. Their time-travelling probably explains how a dinosaur could even--

The girl.

Oh, dead. Dead.

Not important.

Molly Hayes, the youngest. Mutant strength.

Alex Wilder was also a casualty, so of the Pride's children that leaves only the alien:

Karolina Dean. Flight, some sort of cosmic energy... we're still looking into that.

That's totally her. That's totally She-Hulk.

Victor, we don't have a lot of other options.

I'm not gonna talk to this guy. I'm just here if things get ugly.

Things *are* ugly. They're all ugly.

Is somebody gonna deal with She-Hulk having scampi like three tables away?

I just don't want you pawing me when you look like that.

My love, we have to show *strength* here. My male form is more intimidating.

That's sexist.

And the man we're meeting isn't?

She-Hulk has the fakest boobs I ever saw.

And those aren't scampies, they're shrimp.

Vic, you gotta check this out. I'm not into muscles but, I'm, now I'm sort of into muscles.

Is she gonna be a problem, being here? Wasn't she an Avenger?

What's she gonna do? We're just having dinner.

Yeah, but isn't this guy we're meeting supposed to be the most evil person in the whole...

...stuff?

Children.

Kingpin.

"Mr. Fisk" will be fine.

Mr. Fisk. You know who we are?

I'm having dinner with you, at my expense, at my restaurant.

Skip the remedial questions or have someone else speak for the group.

'86 Chateau Lafitte and another round for the children.

You can stop calling us that any time, Shamu.

We represent the Pride.

But there *will* be a lesson.

Please, make a play.

If there was going to be violence at this table it would be over and you would be dead.

You underestimate us.

Never. That's how I stay alive. I'm as aware of your considerable strength as I am of your weaknesses.

You don't want to take this to that level.

Or you'll what, *eat* us? We got *crazy* powers here, not to mention She-Hulk's in the house.

That's not She-Hulk.

The bodybuilder chick? Nice try.

That's not She-Hulk.

Dude, she's *green!*

This is New York.

I think it would be preferable if Miss Hayes shut her eyes for a bit.

Several months ago Mr. Stein and Ms. Minoru encountered a street-level thug who called himself "Pusher-Man".

You duped him into thinking he had an "in" with the new incarnation of the Pride.

Excited, he brought this information to an associate, who brought it to me.

His error was clear to me.

What I'd like you to note is the *manner* of his death, the time taken, the pieces removed, before he succumbed.

This man had powers as well.

Now whether you purport to be the new Pride, or are touting your prowess at having ended them, you all know this:

I will go where you will not. That is why you'll lose.

You're not the Pride. You're a group of kids on the run who want a place to hide.

I'm going to do you that favor.

And you will do one for me.

...and Nico can show him who's boss.

Regret?

It is my meat and drink.

My air, my everything.

The faces fade, the names get jumbled, but regret...

...regret never ages.

The children will come.

They will play their part-- oblivious, just like Fisk.

I suck so hard.

This isn't your fault.

Victor's right: I totally folded in that meeting.

The Kingpin *targeted* you. You go after the strong ones first--that's, like, the first rule. He shook us *all* up.

I think Xavin has a crush on him.

*Uchh.* She's such a *guy* sometimes...

Is she?

I mean... does she really change, or...I mean, as a Skrull was he-- she born with...

...please make me stop.

It's hard for people to get.

We do, but when she's alone with me...

You guys just seem to see things really differently.

But is that real? The real her?

What are you doing?

No! I'm sorry--

Xavin found out I was gay and didn't so much as blink. She's not *pretending* to be a woman; she's learning to be a *human*.

She's trying to change. Become better. You see anyone else making that effort?

I just--

She doesn't fit in, great. Isn't that what this group is supposed to be all about?

I'm not trying to get between you guys. Xavin's cool--

She's more than that.

She gives me something you can't.

"I promise to
be gentle."

THOOM!

Gnntl?

It was
a precision
landing.

"Gentle" means
"We didn't break
the roof".

CCCRRRREEEEEE

Uh... Damn...

I'm watching, I'm learning...

Honey?

Need a minute here...

If she's the Fantastic Four, why doesn't she just use Invincible Woman powers to make a force-field bridge?

I told you like ten times to stay out of my stuff.

But we're heisting! Why couldn't you wear normal-person stockings anyway? I'm gonna have waffle-face.

Just a couple more seconds, honey...

Buncha old junk. You sure about this place?

I think so. Yes.

I mean, isn't rent in New York insane? No way this is just somebody's attic.

Yeah, I'm feeling a massive security matrix. Lasers, alarms...lotta backup systems. I can't manipulate this.

All I can do is blow it out. It'll probably alert the police.

Or possibly S.H.I.E.L.D....

We'll be long gone.

Blow it.

This way.

You're sure?

Everybody stop asking me that.

We totally Shadowcatted! Chase is gonna be so jealous!

Yeah, where is he?

Chase?

Honey, lights.

Right.

Not in Leapfrog... He should've come straight back!

Guys...

He was right in the middle of it.

Chase?

Lace?

...but I totally want that on my tombstone.

CHASE!

You know, not *today*, but...

I underestimated you.

You underestimated *Lace,* Bro-Ho.

I just freaked and jumped like a dope, I was destined for splathood, so scary. And then Lace...

But...

Lace fully dives down, gets a piece of me and snags the wall, she's sliding down it, just cutting through stone, hanging onto my sorry butt--

But that's just... exactly what I...

--it was a *ride,* man. And all over this little guy? Let me see.

The Kingpin hadda know we'd figure this out. He's playing with us.

And he expects us to hand it over to him.

We don't, he'll probably kill us pretty horribly.

I have a plan. Let Molly hit him.

I'm not hitting anybody else that doesn't have powers.

Especially when they've got glands.

One more complication. Can I just have a do-over for the last two days?

We could have avoided all of this if I thought ahead a little.

Regret is a luxury.

Then meet the richest people on earth.

We're here, it's now, we gotta deal. Just think it through...

"...and hope we catch a break."

I'll get the food. You guys grab your stuff.

How long till we're supposed to deliver?

--ninja.

He said be at his office by first light. We got just enough time to hop out of state till we figure out what we're gonna--

That's a lot of ninjas.

It's a bunch.

That's more than the usual amount of ninjas.

Why my client paid such an outrageous fee to have you steal something that in every sense belongs to you, I cannot say.

What's important is that you have it. And I need it.

Hence the ninjas.

It's some kind of energy amplifier, right? For what, a bomb? Hyperspace travel? A super-soldier formula?

We at least get to know, right?

You get to live.

That's good enough.

We're a hundred years from home.

THE NEW YORK HERALD.

WHOLE NO. 24601    NEW YORK, WEDNESDAY, JUNE 27, 1907    PRICE, FOUR CENTS

TYPHOID MARY APPREHENDED
Typhus Terror At An End.

Wow. This is *amazingly* bad.

Should you be sitting? That healing spell--

--worked great. I'm fine, except for the amazingly bad.

"Typhoid Mary." Didn't she fight Daredevil?

We have to get back to our time as soon as possible.

Our time where men are attacking us with missiles and ninjas?

Yeah, we were like three seconds from being blown to bits, which I've sort of had enough of.

As usual, you're missing the bigger issue. What you should be worried about is the Butterfly Effect.

Dude, I'm totally on top of the Butterfly Effect!

What were they, like, bigger?

I don't think it'll be a problem--which is the good news, since we're going nowhere.

But if we mess with the time stream, don't we end up never being born, or Hitler won, or something?

Well, if the... what is it, Yorkes? Gert's parents--if they were time travelers they'd have to have some kind of fail-safe, some protective bubble or something to keep them from effecting major change, or they'd never come back to the same future twice.

They'd also have to have a power source good for a round trip. We can't assume anything is working in our favor.

We also can't hide in an alley and do nothing.

You're not even pretending to contain your excitement.

How often do we get this chance? A world we've never seen!

You've seen many worlds--

But this is our planet. Our history. We're living in history.

Right. We're living in something I flunked. How do we make it go away?

Inky.

I vote spell.

Moll with the call! Staff up, Minoru.

Yeah, if it goes wrong--

That's a big order...

There's guys in knickers out there. Seriously. I'll cut you.

HOLD-RECORDS INDICATE I AM IMPERVIOUS TO SPELL-CASTING.

NEGATIVE.

Wait a sec. "Holo"?

Can you--

ACCESSING.

There's the little #&$%er.

This'll spot-weld the housing in.

I'm not familiar--

Ah, it's quasi-sentient. Just hold it close.

A frog? I wouldn't have expected such a whimsical design, Victor.

Blame Janet. But it'll go where a plane won't--it's good in a jam.

So are these. Dale and I still can't muster up the big time jumps, but these are perfect for quick escapes.

How far back can they go?

Hello?

Is somebody here with me?

Turn it off.

All right, we heard them. There might be another one of those things somewhere.

It would be in Los Angeles, surely?

There wasn't any Los Angeles worth mentioning back then. Now.

The one we found was in New York--it could be sitting there right now!

Building wasn't that old. But the Yorkes traveled a lot, not just in time.

Trying to find another device is our best shot.

Yay. I mean, I'm all about the mission, but yay.

Killer spell, Nico. I'm sweating so much I *know* we blend right in.

I just wish I'd had time to sew them. I am getting so many ideas from this era...I mean, look at those boots!

...because of the mission.

You sure Old Lace'll be cool in that alley?

Nope. But somebody's gotta watch the frog. Even while it's invisible?

I didn't say *"watch over the frog".* I said watch it.

This cannot stand! Sweatshop owners are Tsars of New World! This very building--

I don't think Leapfrog meant to freak you out. *I* certainly never --

It's not you, man. Frog's calling its own shots. I mean, why didn't it show us that stuff *before* we time-boogied?

UNFAIR UNSAFE UNETHICAL

SWEATSHOPS ARE SLAVESHOPS

WOMEN & CHILDREN AST?

How much of that thing is just my dad?

FWOOSH!!

Uh, our cover..?

AAAAAAHHH!!!

Force-fields on the people up there!

Chase, get Molly to make some new exits and help with debris!

Vic, if there's any metal collapsing, secure it.

I'm gonna talk to the fire.

They're all children...

Anybody else? Can anybody hear me?

Huh?

Hey! Are you okay?

"We can't stick around and get noticed."

At least nobody had a camera. Unless...do they have cameras now?

Yeah, but not on their phones or anything.

If I might ask...

...where do you expect to be going?

Mercy, I was in a state! Welcome! Look at you all--from everywhere!

Lillie McGurty, "the Spieler". Can dance on air, if there's a tune handy.

What's *your* history?

Victor. Cyborg.

I never been to Spain myself. You're all of you Wonders?

Yep.

Nope.

Tristan! Get down here, y'big idiot!

A few of the other Street Arabs...

Small one's *Creeper*...

...*Hoyden* is the lady...

...our most notorious member, the *Yellow Kid*...

...*Dead George Pelham*--has a thing for brains, but a true-blue pal and hell in a tussle...

And the hideous-looking monstrosity with the wings...

Tristan. Pleasure to meet you all.

We got a room for you, all your own. Some grub and a night's rest is what you need.

We have to talk.

Alone, Nico.

Lillie? You gonna leave me alone up there or can you manage another whirl?

*This* is the *girls'* side! No boys are allowed on this side of the room for smooching or any other gross stuff that I can usually hear even when we're not in the same room.

I just worry about you.

I'll be fine.

We have to get out of this time as soon as we can.

Which is why I don't wanna miss this chance. I'm just gonna look around.

Have fun. And then stop having fun and come back.

I'd kiss you if you were a chick.

No smooching means you two, too!

That's all? He gave you that message and let you go?

He said I'd know who and when to give it. I don't see how...

I don't even know what it *means*. But running into him again can't be a coincidence.

And what the hell happened...happens to his face? Do we cause that? No, 'cause then we would have...

*Madre de Dios,* this time-travel logic makes my circuits short.

Yeah, I smelled something burning when you met Miss Dance-On-Air, too.

What, Lillie? Please, she's clearly into Tristan.

That... wasn't the right response, was it?

Wow.

Ties! Ties and stiff white collars!

And wow.

Also, wow.

Excuse me, miss?

May I escort you somewhere?

Oh, I'm fine, thank you.

Come on. I've got rooms, and plenty a' dust--more than you'll make out here.

Hey!

Don't be coy; it doesn't suit.

A girl out alone at night's looking for one thing only.

And that's what I got right here.

If you can't sell them, they hef no use!

But... they will die...

Of course they die! You cut them, you sell them, they die so people will buy more!

You don't sit around admire them when you are losing your job and the butcher won't take our credit!

For the whiskey you paid cash.

Do you want me to show you whose house this is?

No sir.

You keep mouth shut unless I want it open! Understand?

Yes sir.

Should throw you in street.

Tomorrow you find new job. Or maybe I sell you.

What's the matter? Don't you trust me?

The only reason anyone trusts you is that stick.

So yes, I trust you. But it bothers me that I do.

I seen these kids in action and I'm telling you, they're the genuine article.

I coulda gone to the Upward Path, they're sniffin' for recruits but I sez "No, get to the Mineola, talk to Maneater; he'll treat you square."

And what's your idea of square?

Finder's fee, plus a remembrance for any job they pull...

...maybe a word in for me with...you know... the Others?

You don't say their names. They never hear yours. This ensures your continued existence. You're close to crossing a line here that you must not cross.

They don't call me Maneater for any reason other than the obvious.

If there's really a war coming, these kids are gonna tip the scale.

I come to you in good faith, I get threatened with ingestion.

In good faith I came.

Hunh.

Come in.

Forgive me for interrupting.

Not at all.

We have word of a new gang of Wonders, possibly powerful.

They're holed up with the Street Arabs. Things being as they are, I thought we could use a little muscle.

Well we certainly can't have them falling to the other side.

Absolutely. Recruit them...

The usual procedure?

Wake up, C-sleepy-O! It's late and you're making weird noises!

Whuh? Huh, no I... noises?

Moaning. What were you dreaming about?

Uh... electric sheep?

Ack! Easy on the Thing-strength, honey.

Okay, I've gotten a closer look at the 1907 crowd and you know what our parents were right about? Flossing.

Eat up, friends. Sweet rolls and fresh ham-hocks!

All these new words!

Nothing vegan, I'm guessing...

Knock yourself out.

You *stud!*

We got marching orders, Nico? 'Cause I've been talking with The Swell here...

As I learn you're after a priceless object no bigger than that apple, and in a burg of this magnitude, I figure you got just a few options.

You go to the Merchant's Trust and ask them to open the vaults, which they most certainly will not...

...or you go to the Mineola.

The Mineola?

Private subway train, owned by the very powerful people who run the Sinners.

And who are these very powerful people?

Well they prefer to keep their identities secret.

You cn tll us...

Secret, ah...from me.

But us Arabs job for 'em now and again, and if there's anyone in New York knows where the goodies is kept, it's them.

And their group is called the Sinners because they're solid citizens, right?

Back to business. I think we should split up. It's our best chance of finding a new...the overdrive device.

What happened to the old one?

The overdrive... I tossed it in an alley.

Well that's muffin-headed, you don't mind my saying. Lillie...

If it's a machine at all Professor Duck can make it work--he built Tristan his wings!

Please tell me the guy's a duck.

Nah, he's a Chinee, same as dear Miss Nico here.

Bit cracked, as well. Your best bet's the Sinners, my word on that.

First of all, I'm from Japan. By way of Glendale.

Second, we're still splitting up.

Chase, you and Xavin can check out the Mineola, meet these Sinners. Maybe we can make some kind of deal with them if they've got the goods.

A deal? Didn't we just *leave* that party? With rockets on our ass?

You wanna party like it's 1899, be my guest. I'm going back.

Lillie. Spieler. Whatever you...would you bring someone to see this professor if we got the device?

Glad to help.

Great.

Take Victor.

Nico? Can I slip out for a few hours?

More sightseeing?

No, it's... I need to do something, and...

...I thought Molly could come with.

Yes! *Not* picked last!

What about you?

I'm gonna go to the Merchant's Trust.

And ask them to open the vaults.

And if you don't find work, don't bother coming home!

I promise--

Promise does not warm my belly! Your mother may have spoiled you rotten, little Klara, but she's gone now.

Bring home some money or you'll be gone as well!

Excuse me...

Klara? I'm Karolina Dean, this is Molly Hayes.

We wanted to talk to you about yesterday. At the factory...

I don't want any Union, thank you, the Unions are not good...

If I'm seen talking to you...

It's not about a Union.

It's about your power.

You're a Wonder.

I saw the vines you climbed down. The roses. You made them grow, didn't you?

I know nothing. I have to go.

But we're Wonders too!

Karolina has extra-trestal light powers, and I've got super-strength! Like the Hulk, except I don't get green and all defensive.

I'm called *"Princess Powerful"*, except sometimes the guys call me "Bruiser" which is hurtful, and Karolina's *"Lucy in the Sky"*, which is a song that's probably from around this time and all our friends have cool powers too!

What do you want from me?

Nothing. I just thought you might want to know there are other people like you, and that... you don't have to hide, or let people push you around...

And you should totally join our team!

Molly, we can't just--

Why not? She could come back with us and get out of this smelly time!

There's never been anyone on the team that's my age...

I know, Molly, but...

I mean, do you *want* to stay here with your mean old father?

Mr. Prast? He is not my father.

Wow.

You lads put those scum to rights.

I'll bring down the Spieler.

Oh, look.

Metal.

Open Sesame.

Now how do we dispose of the girl?

I think she needs a serious time-out.

This stuff is getting to her, Xav. Maybe it's the magic...

Working for the Kingpin may have been shortsighted, but that doesn't mean these "Sinners" are necessarily--

Dude, I'm talking about Vic!

He and that Spieler chick are vibing like crazy and Nico practically shoves him into her arms!

I'm the one who notices this? Aren't you a girl part of the time?

Yes, but sometimes I wonder if I'm the right girl.

I thought Karolina wanted to be with Nico, and I... I tried pretending I was--

Niiice...

Well, there's no point in holding on to someone who--

Dude, I'm talking about the train!

Whatdaya got?

Excuse me?

Powers. Specialties. What can you bring me I don't already have?

Ahh, these two is amazing! Show Mr. Maneater how you're amazing.

I don't do tricks unless I get a treat.

You do what I say.

You're not the boss of me, big guy, and you know what? I don't think you're the boss of *you*, either.

The private train is really cool but I can smell the engine in here. I bet it's noisy, too.

The sweet ride's back there, right? So why don't you talk to the people in the papoose and tell them they got *real* business.

It's a good thing I skipped lunch.

CRAKK-AHH!!

Is Gertrude with you?

Gertrude would never waste her time with this ape.

Oh no.

Gert and me never wasted a *second.*

Hey, tell me which is worse? That Gert was in love with me...

..or that she's *dead.*

You son of a—

AUNNH!

We have to go, Chase!

FWII

HURRAAY!!

Ah, glory! What a rumpus!

Didjya see the pikers run?

You people don't kid around...

And you! Tossin' girders about...and did I see you *float*?

Well, you know, I'm a cyborg... I work well with electricity, microwaves...computers, which you won't have for a while...

C'mere.

Mhhff... frrgve me...

Oh, we shoulda brought you here sooner! We just forgot you'd be hungry when you made us both wanna barf.

Brrf?

Well, like we said, where we're from, things are really different.

It's against the law to make someone your age work, let alone get married.

You'd be in school right now.

Yeah, every kid gets to go to school!

'cept us...

...and Dakota Fanning...

When did you find out about your powers? If you don't mind talking about it...

I have always just...I thought that was how plants grew.

Because you asked them to.

On our farm in Bern, I would speak and the crops would listen. But the roses...

The roses would speak back.

My mother thought it was unnatural. She was relieved to find me a husband that was sailing far away. She said I shamed God, and never to speak of my cur...my power.

Mr. Prast is a devout man, but he...drinks. He does not find work.

While you slave away at a factory? Lame-o!

It is not so bad. It is just, when I come home so tired, and then he...I do not enjoy it. My...

...my marital duties.

Oh, my God...

He makes you do *chores*?!?

29

He just *left?*

He took the Yorkes' time-travel device and was gone.

Did he say--

Nothing. Just looked at me with...I think it was regret. Or...

Apology.

I don't think he's coming back.

*Pfft!* He's so coming back. Prb'ly with cool weapons or a thing.

Time machine...?

What about Vic and Nico?

You haven't checked in with them?

I'm telling you, this bunch has put us on Queer Street with the Sinners.

We've had black marks in their book before...

Not like this.

They got a beef with the Higher-Ups--which Maneater'll probably kill me for even seein' 'em.

It ain't that, Dead George. We just gotta keep 'em close till I can find Maneater in a less... maneating mood.

If it's a question of brains, perhaps being eaten...

I say toss 'em out 'fore it gets worse.

I say what Hoyden said, mainly because she said it.

Now now, let's not be impulsive. This could still work to our advantage.

As, perhaps, a deal.

...should be concentrating on getting home, not picking up strays!

Xavin, if you had any concept what this girl's been through...

They're arguing about me.

I know! It's SO awkward!

Oh, you're doing that thing I dislike!

I'm not doing anything.

Crossing your arms and turning away does not mean I'm the one being unreasonable!

I believe you'll find it does.

You're the one who wanted to live in the past! Everyone else-- Listen to me! Everyone else has been trying to find a way back!

Stop grabbing me!

Stop making me angry!

*Everything* makes you angry! You're just a bad mood in the shape of a...

Xavin. Xavin, wow, you just totally lost control.

Well, it hasn't been a very pleasant--

Xavin, *look at you!*

I simply wasn't concentrating... maintaining a false shape does take a measure of effort.

Uh-huh. Yeah.

What has happened that is good?

Dumbo, you girled out! That makes this the real you, right?

I didn't realize that was in doubt.

Well, you're pretty pig-headed. But I gotta tell you...

...you're beautiful when you're angry.

No.

Yeah, they're wicked mushy--

This is wrong. You people are...

Klara!

NNUUUUUGGGHLLL...

Do you think that's the worst you can feel?

My staff isn't even warm.

For Babbage's sake, Witchbreaker, must you treat the child so?

She leads a group of Wonders, holed up with the Street Arabs.

They've already made overtures to the Sinners, so I suggest you deal with *them* and let me get back to my work.

Now, my dear, depressing descendant...

"...let's see if there's another way to hurt you."

Ahhhh... Verrry boring...

Uh, that's a time-traveling device.

No, this is *shell* of time-traveling device. Power source is used up.

Power source is from future. So not invented yet. So boring.

Well, do you have, um, any *other* way for us to get to the future?

Yes! Live very long time! Future come without machine!

HA-HA-HA-HA...

Heh heh...we *all* time machines! Oh, so funny for me...

I'm sorry, Victor... It's not your fault.

But what if you don't find a way? What if you can't get back to your own time?

Would you maybe stay here?

Lillie, I... You're amazing; I never...but it's... ...well, it's not simple.

It is for me.

Really? 'Cause from where I'm standing... (...I mean *exactly* where I'm standing...)

Wait...Tristan? You think we--

You guys seem pretty tight...

"*Tight*"? What's that? You implying I'm some sort of notch-house dove?

Uh, no?

Tristan's like m'brother and that's it.

*He* know that?

Victor, if you're stayin' I'm yours for good and all. That's just how it is.

And if I'm not staying?

Lillie, I'm not planning to stay. My friends and I have to get back to where we belong, and when we do...

...will you come with us?

NO!

But you're just another grown-up.

"It won't be long."

I've pushed up the schedule, as you asked. And pulled in a few old mates.

Ratdog and Goldbrick can clear a neighborhood each his own self, and they don't mind killing.

Absolutely. You're to join them as well.

War don't rage in my city without me getting a piece.

Give them one.

Depend on it.

And war is what we'll make. The Upward Path has been praying for a reason to sweep those streets clean.

He's a good soldier.

It's a pity he'll be caught in it too.

The poorer neighborhoods always burn, Dale, and the riff-raff go up with them.

Let them start their war. You concentrate on finishing it.

Back here!
Please!

A device
that size...
We have
to mesh our
shields.

And it'll
work this
time?

Hey Nico. We were worried about you.

No, I'm great.

Anyone else feel like going home?

Yeah!!! Nineteen-oh-seven is ass.

Molly!

Oh it so is.

Can you really get us back?

No, but the Yorkes can. And I'm pretty sure I can make them.

How did you know-- Nico, where've you been?

Wow. You really were worried.

She wasn't that worried. And you know we're not all here: Chase is gone.

He's a big boy. 'Sides, we could use the extra space.

We're picking up a stray.

Nico...

I don't really feel like chatting right now. You're a toaster and she's a ho.

Now give her the message.

One of the Yorkes.

If they've taken Leapfrog we'll be trapped here!

No... We still have time. But we have to move now.

What about the big war?

Don't worry. It'll still be here when we get back.

Hunnnnh...

Made it... thank you, Lord...

Thank you for protecting me.

I don't understand. A message from the future?

I didn't understand either. But it makes sense now.

Tell me again.

"This is your last dance. Your chance to change your fate. Leave this world for a better one..."

"...or waste your days in regret."

I pulled a few bits out of the overdrive device. Figured they'd show up and try to use it once I took their time-ride.

I miss much?

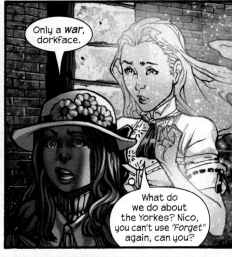

Only a *war*, dorkface.

What do we do about the Yorkes? Nico, you can't use *"Forget"* again, can you?

Why would I want to do that?

The show must go on.

They'll go back to when they came from. And they'll know. What happens to Gert, what happens to them, they'll know every second it's coming.

They won't be able to change anything they do. Or say anything. Not even to each other. For all the world their short, useless lives will play out exactly like they did before. But inside...

...they'll never stop screaming.

Mol... Molly...?

Please...

Klara!

What happened? Who did this?

I'm sorry...

I know who did this.

And I know where he lives.

We don't have time, Kar.

We're all here. This is the time to bail.

What about her?

We bring her with us!

You'll come, right?

You'd... still have me?

Well, you have to not be stupid about gays or freak out 'cause there's jetplanes but *yeah!*

Couple new faces. I can rock that.

Gonna be tight in the frog...

You don't have to be nervous. Time travel's a little weird, but...

I can't.

I can't go, I can't *move*, I'm rooted to the spot Victor I *can't!*

Lillie, you're braver than anyone I know, you just gotta--

*Here* I'm brave! *Now!* In the future? What if I don't like it! What if you don't like *me?*

What if I can't dance?

Lillie, I know you gave me that message. I know if you don't come you spend a century regretting it. *Please...*

If you love me, you'll come.

Don't be scared.

But I was.

I never loved anyone so much, not ever again, and I could be starting my life with him right now.

I sent him to me and still I didn't...how could I be such a child?

A stupid, scared child...

I could have thrived in the present. It would have been wonderful...

I could have skipped all those years wishing... waiting...

...watching the city change in every way that doesn't matter...

...and waiting to send him back. For nothing.

Maybe he failed.

To give you the message.

He gave me the message, Tristan.

He always does.

FWOOM!!?

This is not better!

I didn't just swipe dad's gloves, Xavin.

I studied 'em.

Five minutes till we head back west, peeps. Smoke 'em if you got 'em.

Nobody come into the bushes!

I've had to pee for a *century.*

Sucks that Vic's new girl wussed out at the last second.

You didn't have anything to do with that, did you? Kinda looks like you've got the juice...

You kidding? I practically threw her at him.

Yeah, I didn't exactly follow that either.

Are you really that remedial?

They were in love.

Like, stupid, first-sight, courtly head-over-heels Romeo and Juliet love. Everybody knew it.

What was I gonna do, fight?

I don't know why Lillie chickened out. If I'd felt like that...

But I never have.

I have this, oh, pathological need to insert myself between people...

...which you well remember...

...and I thought I'd try the other thing for once.

Not that it did anybody any good--

I saw Gert.

The time machine took me back to a few years ago, the Yorkes' house...and there she was. On the phone, organizing a protest against...the usual.

You talk to her?

You nuts? She's fourteen-- what do I say? "Hey, in a few years you're gonna find out your parents are evil time-traveling overlords and help kill them, fall in love with the dumbest guy you know and then eat it 'cause he's too slow to protect you?"

You could've brought her back...

Butterfly effect, remember?

Yeah, I looked it up.

'Sides, she had a few good years left. Which is more than I can promise with us.

I just hid. Watched her for a while.

Was it hard?

It was f#%&ing beautiful.

Victor, you know we gotta go.

I just can't figure it out.

It was just too much. Give up the whole world, five seconds to decide...you can't blame her for not going.

Then why didn't I stay?

You stayed with your family.

My family is an evil robot and the liar he murdered.

Sez you, dummy.

Come on.

You know what I liked about last century? No kids.

Nobody treating us like kids. For once we got to be equals, not babies. Could use more of that in the twenty-first. Age doesn't make grown-ups.

That's what my husband always says.

Husband?

Okay. Let's forget I was talking.

We always do. Weirdest part of this for me?

THE END.

# CHARACTER SKETCHES
## BY MICHAEL RYAN

**NICO & CAROLINA**

Darkgrey-Black →

White →

See-through Black →

Edwardian Style.

White →

grey →

Black →

Sleeves/trim lighter than Skirt and Bodice

Brass Buttons →

← Hairstyle only lasts till she lets glow.

Collar Whiter Cream

She'll roll up the Sleeves when she says she's Hot

Two part Skirt.

Not sure How much Color we get in 1907

White or Creme

Brown?

**CHASE**

**NICO**

**MOLLY**

**CAROLINA**

**XAVIN**

**VICTOR**